DRUNK ON YOU

POORVI CHAUHAN

Made with ♥ on the Notion Press Platform
www.notionpress.com

you smell like sundays.

Contents

Contents

Contents

Chapter1

If I could rearrange the earth, all the flowers would spell your name.

Chapter2

How easily you say the words exposing what is true,
I was too busy falling to be sure it was for you.

Chapter3

Since that moment I felt that the world around me suddenly take a vibrant colors I've never seen before as if, I had been wearing a blindfold this whole time.

Chapter4

Look, I've seen a lot of brown eyes but not as much glorious as yours.
I had been in daze,
I wonder,
what kind of smile you wear which makes my feet wander around in so much joy.

Chapter5

Him dancing in the rain,
I can see he has replaced the sun
the world revolves around him.

Chapter6

Claiming to be falling already down,
denying emotions already abound,
clinging to freedom already enslaved,
burning labels already engraved.

Chapter7

I want to be where you are to feel your skin for its scars,
I want to repair your heart with greasy hands and spare parts.

Chapter8

It is so very easy
to open my veins
when love runs deeper than blood.

Chapter9

And while I rest,
he holds the world above for me.

Chapter10

It was midnight,
heavy rain outside,
a heavy heart inside.
Both of us were wet,
before we even met.

Chapter11

If love was like eight hours shift,
I'd work overtime,
just to see you.

Chapter12

It wasn't the moving wind that moved my heart,
but the person
who came along with the moving wind moved it.

Chapter13

Didn't I offer all my love to you from the beginning.

Chapter14

It's not just time that flies when I'm with you, my feet have been off the ground since we met.

Chapter15

If falling in love with you means selling my soul,
I'd pack my bag with noms, take a cab, give a big tip and a high five,
walk gracefully as I knock on your door,
and bring everything I have to offer it all to you.

Chapter16

I'm in love even if its just the shadow of him.

Chapter17

Can I tell you a secret ?
some days, when the sky is in its darkest hue,
and the clouds are light grey blue,
I write poetry,
and its all about you.

Chapter18

If I used my camera as I use my eyes,
you would never run out of pictures of
you,
you
and you again.

Chapter19

I'm drawn to you but I would still be pulled towards you.

Chapter20

For the first time,
I find myself to be so taken by someone so in love,
that it physically pains me,
breathe knocks,
my heart trembles,
my blood rages,
I've become a jumble of sensation
and there's nothing but him.

Chapter21

My love for him feels like liquor but looks like love.

Chapter22

You stole the fire in my chest, just by entering the room.

Chapter23

Wing to wing, eye to eye, you and I, just you and I.

Chapter24

It is I who wrote you letters with no addresses
because each and every word was your name.

Chapter25

He's a written love letter,
in a text messaging world.

Chapter26

When we are together,
fireworks,
that's all you make me feel,
fireworks.

Chapter27

Fortunate are these hands
that get to trace your skin from
head to toe.

Chapter28

Oh baby,
is it not enough that I think about you constantly,
must I also write relentlessly ?.

Chapter29

It's in the night sky and cherry soda and in my favourite books,
I didn't realize how beautiful blue is
until he said it was his favourite color.

Chapter30

Your eyes sank upon seeing me, my day turned into a night.

Chapter31

And at the end of the day, you're the only one I want.

Chapter32

You make me feel like I'm in the 90's romance,
this shall never end.

Chapter33

Who do you think of every time you look at the moon ?

___lowkey you !

Chapter34

There is a song in my heart that only you know the melody to.

Chapter35

Here, under any light,
I find art within his eyes.
As like stars found in the night's sky,
he's a masterpiece no darkness can hide.

Chapter36

They said you're not a poet but with a guy like him,
how can I speak anything less than stars ?.

Chapter37

In a fog of desire, I was his to lose.

Chapter38

I touched his soul,
and scribbled my name on it,
now he'll never get lost again.

Chapter39

They say ;
"people change everyday"
so I vow to fall in love with you every time the sun rises.

Chapter40

Forever still doesn't feel long enough, when it comes to you.

Chapter41

He was like music, and I longed to dance.
His heart was the beat, and I begged for a chance.
His words were the vocals, and I was put in a trance.
His smile was the melody and I fell in love at first glance.

Chapter42

We may have met by accident, but I loved you on purpose.

Chapter43

My love language is saying I HATE you
when what I really want to say is I LOVE you
but if I told you I loved you often as I felt the urge to
you'd think I was nuts.

Chapter44

You didn't give me a reason to write,
you sat your words in my lap,
and I had no choice but to rearrange them.

Chapter45

We sat, a woman passing by said,
“looks like you are made for each other” or “perhaps”
And you said,
“yes we are made for each other” and I gasped.

Chapter46

Once again you have occupied the most forsaken part of my mind,
you don't even know where you belong but you light my whole world.

Chapter47

I trusted a burglar,
he broke carefully in my mind took everything and stole my peace,
I can tell you more about him, but he's out of my world now,
all I can say is he had brown eyes and breathtaking smile.

Chapter48

It's called falling in love
like an accident as if something unplanned, that you can't understand,
but I didn't fall in love with you, I never did,
because we walked in love,
hand in hand.

Chapter49

And it's not love that blinds. Blind are those who never loved.

Chapter50

He's the happy ending not everyone can wait for.

you're my twin flame.

Printed by Libri Plureos GmbH in Hamburg,
Germany